The Pastoral Epistles

A Course Study in Practical Theology

by Dr Christopher Palmer

WIPF & STOCK · Eugene, Oregon

Wipf and Stock Publishers
199 W 8th Ave, Suite 3
Eugene, OR 97401

The Pastoral Epistles
A Course Study in Practical Theology
By Palmer, Christopher
Copyright©2015 Apostolos
ISBN 13: 978-1-5326-6966-8
Publication date 9/23/2018
Previously published by Apostolos, 2015

Course Outline: Pastoral Epistles

Dr. Chris Palmer OMS UK

Description

This course is a study of the three New Testament Epistles traditionally attributed to the Apostle Paul and designated as the 'Pastoral Epistles'; they being 1 and 2 Timothy and Titus. The general purpose of this course is to make the student aware of the issues surrounding the authorship, date and purpose of these three epistles and to allow for a discussion of the principles of early church theology, practice and governance as described within them.

Special attention will be given to the elements of Church practice and policy which are described in order to apply these principles to the 21st century Church. The primary aim of this course is to equip the student with a greater understanding of the work of the Christian minister as they lead the church of God.

This course originally took the form of lectures and seminars first given at an OMS Bible Seminary.

Outline

Day 1	Introduction to the 'Pastoral Epistles' author, date, recipients, purpose, main theology.
Day 2	1 Timothy: The ministry of the local church; a focus on leadership.
Day 3	Titus: The Hope of the Gospel; the central message for the church.
Day 4	2 Timothy: Paul's Last Words; defend the faith in difficult days.
Day 5	Theological Unity? Student seminars on the theology of the Pastoral Epistles.

Recommended Reading

John Balchin, *I want to know what the Bible says about the Church* (Eastbourne: Kingsway, 1979)

G C Berkouwer, *The Church* (Grand Rapids MI: Eerdmans, 1976)

F.F. Bruce, *Apostle of the Free Spirit* (Carlisle: Paternoster, 1977)

Gordon Fee, *God's Empowering Presence* (Peabody MA: Hendrickson, 1994)

Wayne Grudem, *Systematic Theology* (Leicester: IVP, 1994)

Donald Guthrie, *New Testament Introduction* (Downers Grove IL: IVP, 1970)

Donald Guthrie, *New Testament Theology* (Leicester: IVP, 1981)

Donald Guthrie, *The Pastoral Epistles* (Leicester: IVP, 1990)

William Hendriksen, *1 & 2 Timothy and Titus* (London: Banner of Truth, 1957)

William Hendriksen, *Philippians, Colossians & Philemon* (Edinburgh: Banner of Truth, 1962)

I Howard Marshall, *Acts* (Nottingham: IVP, 1980)

Robert L. Reymond, *Paul Missionary Theologian* (Fearn: Christian Focus, 2000)

John Stott, *The Message of Acts* (Leicester: IVP, 1990)

John Stott, *The Message of Ephesians* (Leicester: IVP, 1989)

Derek Tidball, *Skilful Shepherds* (Leicester: Apollos, 1986)

Philip H. Towner, *The Letters to Timothy and Titus* (Grand Rapids MI: Eerdmans, 2006)

Peter White, *The Effective Pastor* (Fearn: Christian Focus, 2002)

Examination

The Course will be examined by means of classroom presentation, essay and research project. The students will complete the following essay title:

Discuss the approach of the Pastoral Epistles to one of the following theological issues: Christology; Pneumatology; Church Leadership; Christian Life; Missions or Authority of Scripture.

Students will **ALSO** complete a research project in relation to their home church situation regarding the issue of discipleship:

Construct an outline for a discipleship course for use in the local church. Examine:

1. *What is discipleship?*

2. *Necessity of discipleship*

3. *Elements of true discipleship?*

4. *A brief outline of the major areas you would use to teach in a local church setting.*

Class project

On the last day of this course there will be student led seminars when the students will present their findings on some of the major theological themes dealt with in the Pastorals. We will divide the class into groups and each will be given a specific theological theme to investigate. Please use this week to study the epistles and report back as a group to the class on the last day with your findings along with a written summary. It will also be vital that you investigate how the teaching presented in the Pastorals relates to the other New Testament epistles.

Group 1	Salvation and Christology	1 Tim.1:15; 2:4–6; 2 Tim.1:9–10; 2:8–13; Titus 2:11–14; 3:4–7 Christology: 1 Tim.6:14; 2 Tim.1:10; 4:1, 8; Titus 2:11, 13; 3:4.
Group 2	Gospel and Mission	1 Tim.1:10; 2 Tim. 4:3; Titus 1:9; 2 Tim. 2:15, 18; 1 Tim. 2:1–7; 2:5–6; Titus 1:1–3; 1 Tim. 3:7; 5:14; 6:1; Titus 2:5, 9; 3:2, 8.
Group 3	The Holy Spirit	1 Tim. 3:16; 4:1; 2 Tim. 1:7, 14; Titus 3:5.
Group 4	Church Leadership	1 Tim. 3:15; 1:4; 3:4–5; Titus 1:7; 2:2–3:2; 2 Tim. 1:8; 2:3; 4:5. 1 Tim. 4:6–16; 6:12–14; 2 Tim. 1:6–14; 3:10–17; 4:1–5.
Group 5	Authority of Scripture	2 Tim. 3:16; 4:4; 1 Tim. 5:18–19; 2 Tim. 2:19, 1 Tim. 2:8, Titus 2:14.
Group 6	Personal Conduct	1 Tim. 2:2, 9; 4:12–16; 6:6–11; 2 Tim.1:5; 2 Tim. 2:2–6, 21–26; Titus 2:11–14

Structure for the project:

1. Introduction – what is the title of your project/subject?
2. Define your subject.
3. Examine the Pastoral Epistles text on the subject.
4. Cross reference with other biblical text.
5. Conclusions: why is this subject important, what can be learned for today?

Contents

The Pastoral Epistles: Introduction

Pay close attention to yourself and to your teaching; persevere in these things, for as you do this you will ensure salvation both for yourself and those that hear you. (1 Tim. 4:16)

This verse could be recognised as the key to understanding the three letters traditionally known as the Pastoral Epistles: 1 and 2 Timothy and Titus; it reveals the author's desire for his readers to concentrate on the personal pursuit of salvation through the gospel and to pass that gospel on to others.

Exercise: Read Psalm 23 and consider the role of the shepherd; his main duties and responsibilities. Discuss how these distinctive features of the shepherd need to be expressed in pastoral ministry.

In order for the church to grow we must know something of the biblical perspectives and directives of church structure, government and purpose; and some of the clearest information on these subjects is found within the Pastoral Epistles. 2 Tim.3:16–17 stands as our reason for depending upon the biblical principles. However we should not treat the Pastorals as a manual for church practice, as there is little instruction concerning administration and worship; there is instead teaching about correct biblical leadership and the necessity to base one's faith and church practice upon scripture.

Many questions have been raised about the authorship, date, recipients and purpose of the epistles; however, it is clear that there are a number of themes which connect the three documents, namely:

1. The Christian's personal conduct.

2. Ecclesiastical leadership and discipline.

3. The importance of sound doctrine and authority of the scriptures.

4. Christology and soteriology.

5. Missions.

6. The Holy Spirit.

Question: Why are these issues essential for the 21st century church?

The purpose of this course is to examine each epistle individually as a piece of literature which was important for the operation of the local church in the 1st century;

and to ascertain what principles could or should be adopted for the church in the 21st century.

Within the Pastoral Epistles we see 3 main areas of concern expressed by Paul:

1. In 1 Timothy: The Ministry of the Local Church (1 Tim. 2:4).

2. In 2 Timothy: Paul's last words to the Church (2 Tim. 4:6).

3. In Titus: The Hope of the Gospel (Titus 2:13).

Pastoral: What's in a Name?

The Pastoral Epistles
In what ways are these three epistles 'pastoral'?

This designation was first promoted by D.N. Berdot in 1703 and was subsequently popularised by Paul Anton from 1726.

However, it is important to note that these epistles are not manuals for pastoral theology, and so the designation simply allows the student to distinguish the group from other New Testament correspondence. Other groups of New Testament literature are: The Gospels, The Prison Epistles, General Epistles etc.

It could be more appropriate to label these three epistles the 'Personal Epistles' and include Philemon in their group, as they are specifically written to individuals and neither to the church in general nor to a particular local congregation (as Ephesians was).

However for the purposes of this course we will confine our attention to the three traditional Pastoral Epistles (PE).

In which ways could these epistles be recognised as pastoral?

1. They were written to new Pastors, Timothy and Titus, as they settled in to pastoral ministry, as inexperienced young men with a major task (1 Tim. 3:15 and Titus 1:5).

2. They were written by a pastor par-excellence, Paul, as he comes to the end of his life and ministry, who is taking his pastoral duties seriously, reviewing his ministry and listing the blessings and difficulties of such a life (Notice how he addresses Timothy and Titus as 'true sons' in 1 Tim.1:2 and Titus 1:4, revealing his pastoral concern for his converts).

The Church is engaged in very serious business; and if we desire to see the church move forward then we need to be serious about our understanding of the word of God. The implications of that word for those of us who are entrusted with the spiritual care of believers in our local church is paramount. The Old Testament prophet Ezekiel records some poignant words in relation to God's view of the leaders of his people; Ezk. 34 provides a warning of the seriousness of the role and also the blessings when carried out by God's prescribed pattern. The overall purpose of the church is to prepare people for the fulfilment of Titus 2:13 – 'looking for the blessed hope'. If this is our purpose, desire and driving force then Church life should be relatively straight forward – but sadly we complicate matters by our petty differences and personal ideas.

> *QUESTIONS*
>
> *1. How would you define the word 'pastoral'?*
>
> *2. What do you think someone needs to learn about the basics of pastoral ministry?*
>
> *3. To whom do you turn for advice and support in ministry?*

Lessons

The Pastorals do contain valuable lessons for the student. It is good practice for the pastor/leader to read these epistles regularly as they do contain some very helpful information, guidance and advice for the on-going ministry of the local church.

1. They provide insights into the operation of some aspects of the early church.

2. They give essential information about the care of people in the church.

3. They give points about church order.

4. They set out the roles and qualities of true leaders.

5. They exalt the Lord as supreme.

As we progress through this course, these important principles will become the objects of our further investigation and discussion.

One aspect which is clear from each of these epistles is the ecclesiastical situation at the time; there was a lot of pressure from false teachers especially those advocating an early form of Gnosticism, asceticism and Judaizers. We will look at these in more depth later.

QUESTION: What issues do you face in your culture in the 21st century?

Application of the biblical knowledge gained is the key to good theological study; accumulating knowledge is of no use unless that knowledge is put into practice in one's particular context. As you read the Pastoral Epistles be sure to apply the knowledge gained to your personal life, situation and ministry.

Authorship, Date and Purpose:

Why write a letter? There are numerous answers to this question; one may wish to pass on greetings to a friend, send information; news or advice. A study of the Pastorals will highlight their author had all these purposes and more in mind when he penned the letters. Traditionally the Pastoral Epistles have been attributed to the Apostle Paul and could be seen as expressing Paul's heart for the church and especially for two individuals who were to follow him in a life of service and ministry. However there have been some challenges to this traditional hypothesis much of the doubt has arisen from the problem of trying to fit the Pastoral Epistles into the Acts framework. Possible answers to the problem include the following:

1. It is possible that the author, Paul the Apostle, wrote these epistles in order to pass on his last thoughts and advice to the two young pastors between 63–65 CE. There is also the possibility that Paul wrote these epistles from Rome during his imprisonment there as recorded at the end of Acts (Acts 28). But since there is no reference to some of the details of the Pastoral Epistles in Acts, there is another possibility—that Paul was released from Roman imprisonment c.65 CE before travelling to Spain and being re-arrested in 67 CE, at which time he wrote 2 Timothy before his martyrdom in 68 CE. A possible timeline for the last years of Paul's life could be:

CE 58   Paul was arrested in Jerusalem.

CE 61–63   This was the period of Paul's first imprisonment in Rome.

CE 64   Paul was released; travelled to Spain and Crete.

CE 64–67   Paul wrote 1 Timothy and Titus from Macedonia.

CE 67   Paul wrote 2 Timothy from Rome having been rearrested.

CE 68   Paul was executed for his faith.

If there was only one Roman imprisonment then all these dates would need to be moved backwards in order to agree with the Acts narrative; with Paul writing all during the period recorded in Acts 28.

2. There is the Fiction theory states that the epistles were written by a pseudonymous author who simply made up the content and put Paul's name on it to give it credence.

3. There is the Fragment theory, which states that an author used pieces or fragments of Paul's writings (which had not been previously published) and expanded them with his own thoughts to make the epistles a fuller document. In this theory, fragments are considered to be genuinely Pauline: Titus 3:12–15; 2 Tim.4:9–15, 20–21a and 22b; 2 Tim. 1:16–18, 3:10–11, 4:1, 2a, 5b–8, 16–19 and 21b–22a. Yet this theory appears particularly doubtful, especially since 2 Timothy is a very personal letter, with references to Paul's own family members. Furthermore, these sections are random fragments having little connection to each other; it would be very odd for someone to have kept these fragments. The theory also supposes that Acts provides a full history of Paul's ministry.

4. The Amanuensis theory states that Paul employed a secretary to write his epistles, a fact which would explanation the variations in style and linguistics between the epistles.

5. It has also been proposed that Timothy and Titus may have written these epistles from their memories of Paul's verbal instruction and addressed them to themselves from Paul in order to give credence to their respective ministries in the local church.

Other Objections to Pauline Authorship

1. It has been suggested that the *ecclesiastical situation* portrayed in the Pastoral Epistles is too advanced for Paul's time and reflects a 2nd century standard. Yet this is not necessarily true, as Paul was endeavouring to establish a new framework for church leadership before his imminent death.

2. The suggestion has been made that Paul had no interest in church government, but this too should be discarded, as we see from other epistles and from Acts 20 that he had a keen interest in the leadership of the churches.

14

3. The objection is made that there was no fixed theological tradition to pass on during Paul's life, so why bother with church organisation? However it is clear that Paul and the other Apostles were endeavouring to set a framework of theological tradition (see Acts 15).

On the whole there is nothing to detract from the traditionally held view that the Apostle Paul wrote these epistles:

1. There was a definite system of teaching under construction for the churches to follow, which was apostolically authenticated (see Acts 15).

2. This was being communicated to church leaders by the Apostles and their representatives.

3. Ordination of church leaders was already taking place.

4. There was a developing system of church government.

5. Paul and Apostles were ecclesiastical architects, laying foundations for future development.

As we progress through this course it will become clear that there is a great deal of material in these Personal letters to indicate Pauline authorship; it is especially important to read Acts 20 and the epistle to the Ephesians in conjunction with the Pastoral Epistles, since these relate to the local situation that Timothy was facing as pastor of the Ephesian church. Sadly we have no insight into the beginnings of the church in Crete; the Acts narrative mentions Paul's brief visit as a prisoner in Acts 27, en-route to Rome. However there is no indication that during this time Paul planted a church; it could be suggested that this is when Titus was left behind to commence his work of 'sorting out' the church. The other possibility is that there is a time period following Acts 28, which is not recorded by Luke, in which Paul sailed to Spain and possibly returned to Jerusalem via Crete thus establishing the church and leaving his protégé Titus to complete the work. Paul was then rearrested and sent to Rome where he faced martyrdom. Much of Paul's instruction to Timothy and Titus is personal—for the Pastor's eyes only—whereas in Acts 20 and Ephesians the church is addressed. This should allow the reader to understand the difference the Pastoral Epistles and other letters, as they are personal and so should be treated differently to a public letter.

Heresy

There is one major concern within the whole aspect of understanding the purpose of the Pastoral Epistles, and that is the growing problem of heresy within the embryonic Christian community.

What is heresy? The Greek word 'hairesis' means 'a choice', and in the New Testament this word has three general meanings;

1. A chosen opinion or course taken by an individual as seen within the thinking of a sect or party (Acts 5:17, 15:5, 26:5).

2. Dissensions arising from diverse opinions/factions/differences (Gal.5:20, 1 Cor. 11:19).

3. Departure from revealed doctrinal truth (Titus 3:10, 2 Pet. 2:1, Acts 20:29, Phil. 3:2).

During the apostolic period, three major heresies began to emerge and it appears that Paul was dealing with these early forms of heresy in some of his epistles. This can be seen in the Pastoral Epistles.

1. Judaizers: These teachers insisted upon the unity of Christianity and Judaism; the gospel is simply the perfected law and Jesus is simply a prophet. These teachers believed that circumcision was necessary to true religious observance.

2. Gnostics: These teachers proposed a Docetic view of Christ, denying the incarnation. This view states that the body of Christ was not real but only appeared or seemed, Gk. 'dokein' – to seem to be real. Therefore the sufferings of Christ on the Cross were only apparent or the Messiah who could not suffer was separate from the person in whom he appeared. If the divine and human are separated the incarnation is deemed to be irrelevant and unnecessary hence the very centre of the Christian faith is undermined. Since they viewed all matter as inherently evil they believed that God would not inhabit a human (evil) body. These teachers also practiced a rigid form of asceticism which prohibited marriage and the eating of certain foods. Later Gnosticism developed the belief that true release from the evil world was only possible through the reception of a special knowledge (Greek - 'gnosis').

3. Syncretism was a blending of Jewish religion and heathen (Greek) philosophy which led to an acceptance of pagan practices.

The basic issue at stake in all of these heresies was their denial of the incarnation of Christ, which leads to his being thought of as either a mere man or some superhuman figure. Paul writes about all of these problems in the Pastoral Epistles.

- ➢ 1 Tim. 1:3–7   false doctrine of Jewish legends.
- ➢ 1 Tim. 1:19–20   'shipwreck their faith'.
- ➢ 2 Tim.2:17   'swerved from the truth' concerning the resurrection.
- ➢ 1 Tim. 4:1–5   doctrines of demons, food and celibacy (see also Col. 2:16–22; Rom. 14).
- ➢ 1 Tim.6:3–5, 20   controversy, wrangling and godless chatter.
- ➢ 2 Tim. 2:14ff.   irrelevant controversies.
- ➢ 2 Tim.3:5   form of godliness.
- ➢ 2 Tim.4:3   teachers with an easy message.
- ➢ Titus 1:10   empty talkers of circumcision.
- ➢ Titus 1:14   Jewish myths.
- ➢ Titus 3:9   unprofitable controversies, genealogies and law.

Why are heresies dangerous?

1. Because they are false and lead people astray in their search for true faith.

2. Because they lead to opposite tendencies from the true balance of the scripture (e.g. asceticism, licentiousness).

Against this theological and philosophical background, Timothy and Titus were endeavouring to lead Christian communities. Paul takes up the challenge of combatting these heresies and by his teaching provides the help these young pastors needed to face the opposition of false teachers. As a result, the churches under their care would flourish and be correctly led in the way of God's truth.

Question: What specific problems do you envisage facing in your pastoral ministry from the current trends in religion and society in the 21st century context?

Exercise: if you had to write a letter to a young pastor what issues would you want to highlight as possible concerns for the church today?

Paul's Heart for the Church

Paul's Personal Call to the Ministry

As the Apostle came to the end of his life he recalled this vital element in his ministry—the call of God (1 Tim. 1:12). The emphasis here is on God's work in Paul's life which was dramatic and powerful but also very serious. In Acts 9:15–16 he was told he would endure suffering, and this came to pass (2 Cor. 11:23–33). However in 1 Cor. 15:10 he found that God's grace is the starting point, the continuing strength (2 Cor. 12:9), and the ultimate release in glory (Eph. 2:5–6) because of grace. We are all called to serve in the local church situation! Service was still the driving force for Paul.

If you want to know what someone really thinks, then you must listen to them when 'their backs are against the wall.' Paul was in such a predicament; his life was under threat and so he took the opportunity (possibly his last) to advise and direct the fledgling Churches which were under the leadership of Timothy and Titus (Ephesus and Crete respectively). Remember to read 1 and 2 Timothy in conjunction with Ephesians and Acts 20, where Paul deals at length with the church that Timothy is believed to have pastored.

Paul's concern for the church is summarised in 1 Timothy 4:1. It is essential to protect the church against false teachings so that the people of God will flourish and the gospel will have greater impact. In Acts 19; 20:17–38 (especially v.20, 27–32) Paul commands the Ephesian elders to be faithful to the word of God, since there is no other source for our help, encouragement and edification.

So what are Paul's instructions for the Church? As he speaks from his heart he deals with four areas of importance. They are all issues which we should try to excel in and pursue so that the Church may function at its best and grow.

1. **Exalt the Lord** (1 Tim. 1:17 and 3:16). Here we see the God with whom we are dealing. In 2 Timothy 1:7–10 we see the salvation message revealed and in Titus 2:11–14 we see the culmination of all the Lord has planned for us.

2. **Proper conduct** (1 Tim. 2) Here Paul reveals what is the correct attitude of prayer. In 1 Tim.2:9–3 and 4:12–5:25 he illustrates the importance of personal sanctity and corporate concern. 2 Tim. 2:15 speaks of the necessity of diligence in our personal lives and Titus 2:1–10 again deals with personal sanctity. Christians are to be living epistles for Jesus Christ.

3. **Ecclesiastical discipline** For the church to operate at its best it must be well lead; structured leadership is vital, and strong spiritual leadership is essential (1 Tim. 3, 2 Tim 2:3–7, Titus 1:5–9). By strong leadership I do not mean that church leaders should act like dictators, but rather that they need godly and spiritual discernment in order to give a good example to the church and the world.

18

4. ***Teach Sound Doctrine*** The purpose of the church is to stand for the truth of God's word (1 Tim. 4:11–16, 2 Tim. 3:14–17, Titus 2:11–15). Whilst the main responsibility for this belongs to the leaders, pastors and elders (see Acts 20:28), it is also true that all believers must stand for God's word.

Paul's concern for the Church is revealed within these four fundamental areas of Christian living. We will do well if we heed his words so that we may be successful in the Lord's work.

Exercise: Consider your call to ministry/Christian service; what do you envisage to be the major issues you will need to address both in your personal experience and that of the corporate body of Christ?

1 Timothy: The Ministry of the Local Church
Key Verse: 1 Tim. 3:15

- ***Chapter 1***
  - *Greetings and introduction 1:1–2*
  - *Sound doctrine 1:3–11*
  - *God's grace 1:12–17*
  - *Good fight 1:18–20*
- **Chapter 2**
  - *Prayer for all 2:1–7*
  - *Conduct in the church 2:8–15*
- ***Chapter 3***
  - *Overseers/elders 3:1–7*
  - *Deacons 3:8–13*
  - *Mystery of Gospel 3:14–16*
- ***Chapter 4***
  - *Great apostasy 4:1–5*
  - *Good servants 4:6–10*
  - *Personal concerns 4:11–16*
- ***Chapter 5***
  - *Church members 5:1–16*
  - *Elders 5:17–25*
- ***Chapter 6***
  - *Honour masters 6:1–2*
  - *Error and greed 6:3–10*
  - *Good confession 6:11–16*
  - *The rich! 6:17–19*
  - *Guarding the faith 6:20–21*

Introduction

'But in case I am delayed, I write so that you will know how one ought to conduct himself in the household of God, which is the church of the living God, the pillar and support of the truth.' (1Tim. 3:15)

- This is a rich letter written in very personal terms and explaining much to help the young pastor Timothy in order that he may fulfil his ministry. It is personal encouragement from Paul to a young man seeking to make his first steps in church leadership.

-   This is essential reading to all young Christians, especially those in 'full time' ministry. Timothy was converted in approximately 50 AD and had spent twelve years travelling with Paul. 1 Timothy could be viewed as Paul's written summary of his oral instructions given to Timothy when he was with him on his missionary journeys. We therefore have in this letter instruction which relate to the 'post-apostolic' era.

- Timothy was the pastor at Ephesus (1 Tim. 1:3) a church established during Paul's third missionary journey (Acts 18:19 - 19) c.53-57 CE. Acts 20:17-38 further helps the student understand the content of the Pastorals as there Paul is given verbal instructions to the leadership Timothy had to work with at Ephesus.

- Timothy's task was to preach the gospel and teach 'sound doctrine' (1:5; 4:11–16).

- Timothy was obviously facing some difficulties at Ephesus and Paul wanted to help his faithful servant.

- Timothy is a man we should seek to emulate and it is necessary for us all to show his courage and faithfulness in the work of God.

- It is traditionally accepted that the letter was written approx. 62/63 AD, possibly later, either on route to Rome or whilst in prison at Rome. Much of this debate centres on whether or not Paul was released from his first Roman imprisonment as mentioned above.

Main Themes

1.   Encouragement against false teaching (1:3–7, 18–20; 6:3–5, 20–21).

2.   Gives Timothy written credentials (1:3–4).

3.   Gives instructions in church affairs (3:14–15).

4.   Urges diligence in the work (4:6–6:2).

Main Theology

- Sin, Christology, pneumatology, soteriology, ecclesiology, and eschatology, all of these being areas of concern for any pastor as they seek to lead a balanced church forward.

- The main problems that Timothy was facing were probably embryonic Gnosticism and Judaizers, and although this is important we must not dwell on the problem, but the solution, as recorded in 1:8–11, 15, 19; 2:5–6; 3:16; 4:6–7; 6:3–13, 17.

Ephesus

In order to gain a better insight into Paul's words and Timothy's problems a brief introduction to the city of Ephesus is required. Ephesus was an important city of the Roman Empire located on the major trade routes. It was the capital of the province of Asia with a good harbour which aided its growth and importance. As the capital it held important status in the political, economic, and religious arenas with a particular emphasis upon the worship of the goddess Diana or Artemis (see Acts 19). The Temple of Diana was known as one of the Seven Wonders of the ancient world; her worship was idolatrous and involved the practice of magic. Diana was viewed as the mother goddess portrayed by the many breasts on her statue; a huntress; protector of young virgins her worship brought great profits to the silversmiths of Ephesus. Timothy was therefore faced with a number of challenges including: Roman politics, wealth, false religion, worship of a female deity, and black magic.

1 Timothy Chapter 1

It is important for our purposes to always examine the role of the pastor as outlined in the Pastoral Epistles; however it must not be the sole purpose of the investigations, as there is much in each chapter which is relevant to the whole of the Christian Church.

v.1–2 Paul had a particularly good relationship with Timothy; Acts shows that he was a companion of Paul during his missionary journeys. Here he refers to him as 'son in the faith', which is most probably a reference to his conversion under Paul's ministry (Acts 16:1–3). We have a responsibility for others who come under our spiritual influence; and Paul wanted to pass on beneficial instructions to the younger man whom he regarded as his spiritual 'son'. It is vital that we never think that we have or know all the answers; it is important to seek good godly advice from those whom we respect in spiritual matters.

v.3–11 Beware of false teachers; a pastor's heart is here revealed through a concern for the protection of the congregation of which he has spiritual responsibility; the pastor must watch over the people as a shepherd with the flock. But how do we recognise false teaching? The safest course is to be sure of a knowledge of the truth of the biblical narrative and the theology contained within; as the pastor knows the truth so too this can be passed to the congregation hence preparing all to recognise what is false and unbiblical. The pastor should:

1. *Know the true word.*
2. *Pray for direction.*
3. *Remember you have a responsibility to self and others.*
4. *Never teach out of selfish gain.*

v.5 What is the correct motivation for all our work and service for God? It is love! If in our ministries we concentrate on the love of God which is expressed in his word then there will be blessing. Paul highlights this in 1 Cor. 13 the famous chapter on love sadly so often kept for weddings and funerals; however contained in its verses is essential help on understanding love and its impact upon the individual.

v.11 The gospel is the gospel of the glory of the blessed God—it is God's gospel, his mission and his love (2 Cor. 4:4–6). It is imperative to remember that the whole message revolves around God not us! The pastor must never be a self-centred individual but one who's primary role is the spiritual care of those in the community both inside and outside the church.

v.12 Why are you here? This is a vital question to examine (take a few minutes to think around this question and consider your true reasons for attending Bible College or the role you currently have in the local church). Paul here recollects his call to ministry and despite the difficulties faced he is full of gratitude towards God for choosing him to be a bearer of the good news of the gospel. There will be periods of hardship as you serve the Lord; doubts; fears; criticism; questions and despair; however at those times remember who has called you to his service: the Lord 'kurios' the supreme authority!

Are you thankful that God has chosen you to serve him in his ministry in the world?

If you are going to serve in a manner that is in line with God's plans, then you will require:

1. *Strength from God.*

2. *Work for God.*

3. *Goal is God himself.*

v.17 Here we see a picture of the God whom we serve; this is known as a Doxology— an ending of praise to the God we know and serve. In this verse we see that God is:

1. *King.*
2. *Eternal.*
3. *Immortal.*
4. *Invisible.*
5. *Wise/ all knowing.*

(see also Rev. 15:3; Rom.1:23; Col. 1:15; Rom. 16:27).

Church discipline

v.20 To be handed over to Satan means to be put out of the church into the realm of Satan (i.e. the world outside the church); possibly set apart from the church to 'learn a lesson' and understand that God can forgive their misdemeanour. Church discipline is an important issue for the Pastor/leader; how we deal with matters of discipline in the church can affect the whole body of Christ. It is therefore necessary to be firm, fair and biblical in one's approach to disciplinary matters.

Quality Control in the Church:

How are disciplinary matters dealt with by leaders?

There will be times when you will have to deal with serious matters, such as immorality or financial impropriety, and it is essential that you deal with them in the biblical way. The Bible lays down principles for dealing with problematic church members.

Community discipline is essential, and all churches should have a disciplinary procedure in place as part of its constitution. If this is the case, all members should be aware of this policy and therefore will not be able to object when a decision is made.

What is the Framework for Discipline?

1. Brother to brother (Matt. 5:22–24; 1 Cor. 5–6).

2. Two/three witnesses speak to the erring member (Matt. 18:15–16).

3. Pastor/elders speak to the erring member (Matt. 18:17, 1 Cor. 1:11).

4. Excommunication for the unrepentant member (Matt. 18:17, 1 Tim. 1:20, 3 John 1:9).

5. What about being accepted back, after genuine repentance? (Jm.5:19-20)

(See also, Ezra 10:1–18; John 9:22, 34; 2 Thess. 3:6–15; Titus 3:10–11; 1 Tim. 5:20; 1 Cor. 11:30; Rev. 2:20–22).

Serious Issues

Serious matters of discipline will be few and far between, be sure that no one 'lords' it over a congregation, making rules for the most insignificant matters and taking the joy out of discipline. Our preaching and teaching should be enough to encourage people to live as Christians, the emphasis should be placed on good solid biblical instruction, allowing the convicting power of the Holy Spirit to work on people's lives to change them in God's time. Enforced restrictions can sometimes prove negative.

The whole matter of discipline needs to be treated with the respect it deserves; remember not to discuss the 'issues' openly when other people's lives are involved— we are not to be gossips. Discernment is essential in all such matters, for judging others can be a big problem (Matt. 7:3ff.) See also 1 Cor. 4:5; 6:1; 1 Pet. 4:15; Eph. 4:32; Gal.6:1.

Be prepared to act but don't go looking for trouble!

1 Timothy Chapter 2: An Attitude of Prayer

Prayer is a vital and integral aspect of the Christian experience. Without prayer, the individual loses the direct contact with God which is necessary in order to direct their ministry (Matt. 6:5–15). The pastor must be an individual who prays; some advice I once received from an experienced pastor was: 'if you desire to excel at anything in ministry; excel at prayer'. These words are extremely important for the pastor and this advice should be taken seriously and applied to one's personal endeavours.

v. 1–8 Here is the urgent call to prayer for the Christian and especially for the pastor. 'Exhort' means to urge or call upon. The Apostle is concerned that Timothy should pay serious attention to the subject of prayer—no one can afford to neglect prayer; whoever we are, whatever we may know, we cannot progress spiritually without the essential ministry of prayer.

What is Prayer?

- *Supplications.* These are precise requests for specific needs.

- *Prayers.* Prayer is a general term for confessions/adorations.

- *Petitions and intercessions* are prayers said on behalf of others.

- *Thanksgivings.* These are prayers of praise

Why Pray?

There are two main reasons why we must pray:

1. It is for personal benefit; growth, direction and help (Matt. 6:6; 7:7–12).

2. It is for the benefit of others (Eph. 1:15–18; 3:14–21).

Paul says a lot about prayer in his epistles, and here we see that it is necessary to balance in our prayers. The Bible is a book of balance and we must not over-emphasise one aspect of its teaching—including its teaching on prayer—to the detriment of any other. Never get carried away with just one teaching, but be a student of the whole of the Bible's doctrine and tradition (Acts 20:20).

Reasons for Prayer

v.2 Social and political peace; this provides dignity for the soul.

v.3 Provides salvation for others.

v.4 Allows us to participate in the desire of God's heart.

v.5 There is a mediator through which we can to come to God—and that is Jesus; he provides the point of contact between humanity and the Father so that we can participate in the ongoing work of the gospel (Heb.7:25).

Split into groups and examine these references to prayer in Paul's writings; consider in each case where and why prayer is necessary:

Phil.4:6–7; Col. 1:3; 4:2–6; Eph. 1:15–23; 6:18–19; 1 Thess. 5:17; also consider Lk.11:1-4; Mt.6:5-8.

Exercise: write a prayer for your country that covers all these areas of concern.

The Central Calling of the Believer

v.7 To point people to the Lord Jesus Christ. Teaching and preaching are the central ministries of the pastor, but there must be an emphasis on faith and truth.

The Correct Attitude and Conduct in Life

v.8 The believer must have holy hands; this means:

i.   A pure life – what affect does purity/holiness have upon the individual? How much attention do we pay to purity of heart and life? Temptation is a real part of the Christian experience – be careful especially over the following major areas of temptation: sexual, financial, power!

ii.   No disputes – personal attitudes of dispute and animosity can prove to be detrimental to the on-going work of the gospel and does affect the impact of our prayers. Unity is a key biblical principle that we must be sure to uphold within the local congregation – very often this will be affected by the role of the pastor.

iii. Modesty (v. 9).

iv.   Good works (v. 10).

v.   Learning (v. 11).

vi.   Respect (vv. 12–14).

The New Testament says a lot about the role of women; Paul here is making a statement about the conduct of women in the local congregation. This is a thorny issue within evangelical Christianity; thinking ranges from the total suppression of women in spiritual roles within the church to the acceptance of women in any leadership position. The first essential is that men should never abuse the positions of authority they hold within the church. Also it is vital to understand that the gospel is a radical message that allowed women the opportunity to learn when they lived in a culture that did not allow any such learning.

The specific situation in Ephesus must be taken into consideration in this debate; the goddess Diana was the centre of Ephesian worship and this may well have had an impact on the role of women in that society; possibly seen in their very public role within the worship of the female deity. Paul was also dealing with a large Jewish element in the churches; a group to whom women in leadership would have been anti-cultural. The specific reasons for Paul highlighting this issue here must be interpreted in light of other Pauline references to very influential women in the embryonic church. Acts 18:24-28 reveals the important teaching ministry of Priscilla; rm.16:3-5 classes her as a fellow worker with Paul and 1 Cor.16:19 lists Priscilla as leading a church with her husband. Rm.16:1 mentions the key role played by Phoebe a servant or one who ministers to the church in a variety of ways. Rm.16:7 brings commendation to Junias most probably a female involved in public ministry. It is also important to note the OT precedent set by figures such as Deborah Jud. 4:4 she had the role of Judge and prophetess in Israel. I submit it is essential to revisit the role of women in the local church; salvation and the essential person of the Holy Spirit is not limited by gender; hence one must give serious consideration to the role of women in leadership. The embryonic church accepted female ministers, servants and teachers perhaps in the 21st century the evangelical church should begin to look at the subject through fresh eyes and not with preconceived patriarchal traditions?

The debate continues about the roles and responsibilities of women in the church and this is very much affected by cultural differences and concerns.

DISCUSSION: What is your cultural view of women in ministry, especially in pastoral leadership?

1 Timothy Chapter 3: Church Government/Leadership

Exercise: Read Acts 20:17–38. As Paul addressed the Ephesian elders what can we learn about the model Paul envisions for leadership and the qualities of the leaders addressed? Also refer to Psalm 23 and Ezekiel 34 in order to construct a wider picture of the biblical standard of leadership.

Church leadership is possibly one of the most controversial issues facing the pastor; the choice of the wrong people in key positions can lead to severe problems. However, the correct people in the correct positions can make the pastor's role much easier, and lead to greater blessing among the local church congregation. In this chapter the author sets out some helpful guidelines for leadership, especially those qualities or characteristics which should be found within all potential leaders. As you step out into the leadership of churches, be sure to have a deeply spiritual group of fellow leaders who can assist with the ministry and help alleviate some of the pressures you will face.

v.1 A bishop or elder is someone who watches over the flock; who brings care, inspection, visitation; inquiring into the well-being of the people of God. Guardianship is an interesting parallel (see Acts 20:28 and 1 Pet. 5:1–4). Another possible interpretation is 'overseer' or shepherd/pastor; i.e. the one who feeds, nourishes, cares, guides, cherishes and rules the flock (Eph. 4:12).

There is much debate as to the correct interpretation of these words; however it is vital to remember that all those in spiritual authority should have a pastoral care for people. The essence of true church leadership is a heart for God and his people, a compassion which reflects that of Jesus when he was on earth. Many suggest that the following characteristics of leaders should firstly be applied to Pastors, as this is the only description of any teaching church leader set out in detail in the New Testament. One may assume that pastors should be considered as the 'first among equals' and therefore should demonstrate these characteristics. However, it is important to remember that pastors (according to Eph. 4:11) are a gift from God to the church and can have a peripatetic ministry; whereas here in 1 Timothy we are informed about those leaders who should remain within the local congregation when the pastor may move on to another ministry or if due to other circumstances there is no pastor in situ.

v.2–7. The divine prescription for leadership in the local church is given here; there are a number of personal characteristics which should be examined before any person is installed into the office of 'bishop, overseer or elder'. The divine standard is very high and hence it is vital that individuals are examined carefully before being invited to consider joining the leadership of any local church congregation.

i.   They must above reproach from those outside.
ii. They must be faithful in their marriages; a one woman man (does this preclude women?)
iii. They must be temperate and vigilant (watchful) in spiritual things.
iv. They must be sober, not only free from alcohol which deadens the senses but also in terms of their general life style.
v.   Their lives must be orderly; they must be self-controlled and self-disciplined.
vi. They must be hospitable; their homes must be open to all.
vii. They must be able to teach, having biblical understanding with the ability to pass it on to others.
viii. They must not greedy for money, but have a servant attitude.
ix. They must be gentle rulers; not dictatorial.
x.   They must not be recent converts; experience is helpful (new churches need to be watched over by the church planter or another experienced Christian leader in the vicinity).
xi. They must have a good report/testimony both inside and outside the church.

Here we are confronted with the picture of an individual who must be highly spiritual and seeking to serve God; having an excellent character. Questions are often raised as to where these perfect people can be found and this is a question with no easy answer.

QUESTIONS

1. How do you approach the matter of choosing leaders within your local church?

2. Consider the following: an individual feels that he has been overlooked for a position as an elder in your church and he begins to spread unpleasant rumours about you the Pastor. How would you counteract this situation and bring the person to a position where he feels comfortable with the decision made?

Elders

The position of elder is a role that sees its various meanings and ministries set out in the New Testament, it is an important role within the church. The Greek words to describe someone in this position are;

- *'presbuteros' - meaning older*
- *'episkopos' – meaning overseer or bishop.*

The term was derived from those older men in ancient tribal society who were responsible for passing on the traditions of their people, and so the people reading Paul's letters would be well aware of the meaning. Today in the church we see a number of different ideas surrounding elders, but the scripture is clear on certain aspects, especially their 'qualifications' and major duties.

The main texts which show the elder's role are:

1. 1 Timothy 3:1–7

2. Titus 2:5–9

3. 1 Peter 5:2–4

These verses apply to the role of the pastor as well as elder; it is interesting to note that a pastor, although 'called' by God to the ministry and known as a shepherd, is really an elder. In some churches it is possible that this position is a paid one, but this is not essential, as a layperson can fulfil the role. Their distinctive role is the ability to teach. Paul's words to the Ephesian elders in Acts 20:17–38, are essential reading for those entrusted with spiritual leadership in the church.

Deacons

vv.8–13 The second group of leaders dealt with in 1 Timothy are deacons or servers/helpers. It appears that their priority is to free the pastor and elders to be involved in the more spiritual ministry. Much of the characteristics required for this role are the same as those of the bishop/overseer. Many accept the 7 almoners as chosen in Acts 6:1–4 to be the precursors to these particular leaders. Yet although they have a more practical ministry, they too should be spiritual people.

v.14–15. The writer is keen to ensure that the church of God is correctly led as the type of leadership a church has reflects not only on the church but also on the Head of the Church: Jesus Christ. It is essential for us to recognise that the church is bigger than any individual, and that all people are simply servants of God involved in his work in his church for his glory.

v.16. Here we are reminded of the reason why we are involved in the Christian ministry; it's all about the Lord, the Son of God, who became the saviour and has commissioned us to serve him in this generation.

The word deacon comes from the Greek word 'diakonos', which means 'servant. Deacons are introduced to the scene of Acts quite early on in the story. It is generally accepted that the men chosen to serve 'on tables' in Acts 6:1, were the first deacons, although these had specific duties and can only be seen as an early form of this office. Their primary function was to look after the communal affairs, or the practical matters, within the early Christian community in order to allow the Apostles to spend their time praying and preaching (Acts 6:4).

These men had to fulfil certain criteria before appointment:

1. Honest report.

2. Full of the Holy Spirit.

3. Having wisdom.

4. Practical people.

5. Men of faith.

Notice that when the church was correctly organised, the word of God spread (v. 7).

The other scripture reference to deacons can be found in 1 Tim. 3:8–13, where a fuller character description is found. Note these are character traits rather than spiritual abilities; the latter are required for pastors and elders.

1. Grave/reverent.

2. Not double tongued – saying one thing to one person and a different thing to another.

3. Not much wine – or dependent upon alcohol.

4. Not after filthy lucre; not in it for the money.

5. Able to defend the faith and preserve truth.

6. Must be examined and if found blameless can do the job.

7. One wife – faithful.

8. Good home – run along Christian principles.

Every Christian should adopt the attitude of a deacon and serve, whether they are a pastor, Sunday school worker or church cleaner.

The role of the deacon's wife ('deaconess') is also raised by Paul in order to show how important the home life is, and that very often a 'team' effort is necessary. The words 'she should be' are thought by some to indicate that deacons wives should be called deaconesses. In any case, the deacon's wives are to be:

1. Grave/reverent.
2. Not a slanderer or gossip, not guilty of defamation of character.
3. Sober in spirit.
4. Faithful in all things – dependable.

Another Look at Leaders: The 'Must-Be' People (1 Tim. 3:13)

Biblical leadership in the church is essential, and sadly the debates about leadership have caused people to turn away from the important issues of following God's will and concentrate instead on man's thoughts. Note that in chapter 4:1–3 Paul warns that human thinking is contrary to God's ways. Why do we think we know better than God? So leaders – the MUST BE PEOPLE! 1 Tim. 3:2, 8 and Titus 1:7 show that God's standard is high—but it is there for a reason. God desires leaders whom he can trust to lead the flock of God in his direction and not theirs (1 Pet.5:1–4 which is supported by the further text of vv. 6–9 within the context of elders/leaders and examples).

Acts 20:17–38 also explains Paul's thinking on this subject. The shepherd is to feed and defend the flock, and this can only be achieved as the under shepherds learn from the Good Shepherd. The two main local leaders are elders (those with the spiritual authority in the church) and deacons (who have no real authority but are servants of the church). Pastors are not included in this study as they are a gift of Christ to the church (Eph. 4:11).

New Testament church organisation is a vital subject: Jesus chose 12 to be with him and to preach; the 11 chose 1 to make up the 12 after Judas' demise; Paul installed elders and Titus and Timothy had to carry out the same task. Note that leaders can expect the greater judgement for their work for they are representing God before the people. James 3:1 says that 'didaskalos' ('teachers') receive greater judgement due to their great influence. Church leaders must be spiritual men who answer to God and are accountable to the congregation for their words and actions.

This is a further step in the same direction of Romans 12 and 1 Corinthians 12–14 where God has placed certain people in the local church to carry out the purposes of God in the congregation—leaders are one such group. So what MUST LEADERS BE? Rather than get bogged down in unnecessary arguments about the role of leaders, here are some principles by which leaders should operate.

1. They must be of exemplary character (v. 2, 7–8) both outside and inside the church! 'Above reproach' means above blame in the community, holding a good reputation. What people see of us outside is vital, as the positions of leaders (elders and deacons) come under more scrutiny since people associate the church with its leaders!

   The Christian leader must be faithful in his home life, and towards his associates and friends, work colleagues and family. This earns respect for his position in Christ! This must also be attained by the correct use of authority and the control of one's own desires, in particular the control of his tongue, as gossip has no place in the leader's life. Gossip stirs up trouble and contention, or destruction in word or deed, must never be part of leader's ministry. Leaders are to be 'blameless'—*do you still want to be an elder/deacon?*

2. Of spiritual character (v. 2, 5, 6). Both elders and deacons must be spiritually minded (Acts 6:3), but there is one major issue which separates the elders from deacons. In verse 2 it says that elders should be 'apt to teach' i.e. they must know about the things of the kingdom and be able to pass that knowledge on in a sensible and helpful manner both publicly and privately.

   There is no need for a deacon to be expected to preach/teach—but some can, and others without position should be encouraged to do so too; elders are expected to be able to teach the people, and when there is no pastor they should take the spiritual lead as regards doctrine and ministry. Note that (v.6) elders should not be new converts due to lack of understanding; power can corrupt. Moreover, in v. 10 we see that deacons should prove themselves before being given position.

3. Recognising the lordship of Christ (v.16). All leadership issues are dealt with easily if the sentiments of verse 16 are accepted—Christ is the head of the church and we are all merely servants of the living God.

The wrong people being installed in leadership has caused many problems in churches, but this need not be so if we follow the Bible pattern God will bless his church.

Church Organisation

Most churches are organised by the Pastor, elders and deacons (usually including treasurer and secretary). These people are the ones entrusted to the day to day affairs of the church. Generally speaking, the pastor and elders are more concerned with the 'spiritual' matters and the deacons with practical issues. There are, in some countries, boards of trustees who have responsibility for financial matters, especially to stand as a 'guarantee' for any major debt incurred by a church.

The major church officers have to come up to the standards as laid out in scripture, remember:

1. The pastor is a gift of Christ to the church (Eph. 4:11), called and equipped by God for the work (Eph.4:12).

2. Elders must have the qualifications listed in 1 Tim. 3, Titus 1 and 1 Pet. 5; these are strict and should be adhered to in order to meet the divine blueprint for the church.

3. Deacons (probably including treasurer and secretary), have their qualifications listed in 1 Timothy 3.

4. What about youth leaders, Sunday school teachers etc.? Although there are no direct 'qualifications', we must remember that all these positions require true Christian character and commitment. Ultimately we are all called to be 'salt' and 'light' and should therefore seek to emulate the highest possible spiritual standards.

In this area we must realise that authority in church life must be first and foremost spiritual. Remember that we are a spiritual community, hence the pastor and elders should have ultimate responsibility for all decisions in church life. Other servants should be there simply to carry out the decisions made by the 'spiritual heads,' Acts 6:1–7.

Three Main Types of Church Organisation

1. Episcopal – a church governed by bishops.

Greek: 'episkopos' meaning 'overseer' (Acts 20:28, Phil. 1:1, 1 Tim. 3:2).

Greek: 'presbuteros' meaning 'elder' (Acts 20:17, 28).

The main bodies governed this way are Roman Catholic, Church of England and some Methodist churches.

2. Presbyterian – church governed by a presbytery or board of elders (Acts 15, the Council at Jerusalem, is the standard used here, also 1 Tim. 4:14). Two kinds of elders form a presbytery:

   a) ruling elder – possibly a layman.

   b) teaching elder – pastor/clergyman – probably paid.

The main bodies governed this way are Presbyterian churches and Reformed churches.

3. Congregationalism – church is governed independently with the autonomy of the local congregation.

Greek: 'ekklesia' meaning a wider body of believers, meeting together in a local assembly. This style emerged under the Puritans in 17th century England.

Main bodies governed this way are Congregational, Baptist, Brethren, Assemblies of God.

1 Timothy Chapter 4: Good Discipline

vv.1–5 Apostasy is a deliberate rejection of the faith after an initial profession of faith. Here the reader is warned about the prospect of many people being affected by false doctrines e.g. i) the prohibition of marriage; ii) abstaining from certain foods.

It is essential that the Christian is properly equipped to deal with the possible false teachings in the church. Ephesians 6 describes the whole armour of God which is at our disposal. The pastor is the key figure in setting the local church on the correct spiritual path.

Exercise: What is your understanding of the role of the pastor? Spend a few minutes writing down your thoughts and key words that describe what you perceive as relating to pastoral ministry.

vv.6–16 The role of the Pastor.

   1. Preach the truth to prevent apostasy.

   2. Present sound doctrine.

3. To be disciplined in life.

4. Need to teach not simply exhort/encourage.

5. Be an example to all in:

   i)   speech

   ii)   conduct

   iii)   love

   iv)   faith

   v)   purity

6. Scripture must be central.

QUESTIONS

How can the areas listed above be made more effective in your life and ministry? The answer to this question depends on your understanding of pastoral ministry.

1. What do you consider to be pastoral ministry?

2. How do you envisage your future in ministry?

Take some time now to think this issue through in your personal situation.

v.15 Meditate/ take pains. This means to be completely absorbed in the spiritual matters that are the heart of Christian ministry. These are the most important issues with which any individual can be involved. This will have a great effect on others as they see your faith in the life you live before them and a true Christian character.

v.16 Pay close attention, be eager not to let the standard slip in terms of:

   i.   your own spirituality;
   ii.   your teaching;
   iii.   your determination to persevere;
   iv.   your salvation.

The area of the pastor's personal devotion is essential, for first and foremost the pastor is a disciple of Jesus Christ and as such should be a committed Christian following all the regular means of grace available. It is only as the pastor sets a good spiritual example that he can expect his congregation to follow and grow in spiritual things.

1 Timothy Chapter 5: Widows and Elders

vv.1–16 Here Paul deals with the matter of the care of widows in the local church; which was a problem in the ancient world.

1. Widows were neglected and left to die a lonely death.

2. Author reminds of one's responsibility for humanity.

3. Social aspect of the gospel.

4. Also possible help in finding another husband v. 14?

The early church confronted the issue of practical or social ministry from its commencement as recorded in Acts 6:1-8. There was a practical concern for the daily needs of the widows in society; they had no access to government aide as is the case in many places today hence the church had to step in to meet the needs. Food given on a daily basis came from the believing community and helped to support these outcasts of society.

The issue of one's engagement in the social gospel is important. The church must have a social awareness and there are a variety of means of engagement with social issues. It is not good practice to simply tell a starving man the Jesus loves him; the man may well need salvation but his immediate need is food. James reminds his readers of this responsibility Jm.2:14-26. Good works are not the means of obtaining salvation but they should be a natural result of hearts that have been changed by the gospel.

Exercise: Consider your local church setting; what social needs do you see in the community? What action could you the local church community take in order to alleviate the situations highlighted?

vv.17–25 Elders:

1. Same as bishops in chapter 3.

2. Financial help for their ministry is acceptable (are these to be seen as full time pastors?).

3. v. 20 Any leader who openly sins must be prepared for public rebuke. The church must be pure and its leaders are the prominent and public measure of the church—if the leaders fail then the church, gospel and the Lord are also brought to disgrace.

v.23 This is a personal piece of advice for Timothy possibly due to a consultation with Luke, a travelling companion of the author. Timothy was a timid individual and here we see that he had some kind of stomach complaint – maybe an ulcer from the stress of leadership! Paul highlights the poor sanitation and lack of good clean drinking water and allows Timothy to drink a small amount of wine which has certain medicinal properties. Many use this as a proof text to allow the free consumption of alcohol; beware the use of eisegesis i.e. taking any text to prove your personal desires. Alcohol is seriously addictive and can cause untold problems to health and family life. This is why Paul cautions the Ephesians in Eph. 5:18 to avoid drunkenness as this can lead to all forms of debauchery and licentiousness as its effects dulls the senses and leaves the individual exposed to all kinds of unfortunate misbehaviour. Gen.9:20-29 Noah acted indecently due to the effects of wine; Gen.20:30-38 Lot was abused by his own daughters through excess wine. (Prov.20:1; 23:20-21, 29-35).

So why does Paul recommend a little wine? I believe that here we are confronted with three important issues surrounding sickness, health and healing them being:

     a.   *The Christian is not free from sickness 2 Tim.4:20.*
     b.   *Medicine is there for ones benefit Col.4:14 Luke was known as the 'beloved physician' and was a companion of Paul.*
     c.   *There are both natural and spiritual answers to sickness Jm.5:14.*

There is much debate as to the role of divine or miraculous healing in the 21st century church; many reject its role. However within the biblical narrative one is confronted with a God who heals both OT and NT relate many incidents of individuals being healed. Spiritual healing or restoration is the most important aspect however one should never dismiss the possibility that an omnipotent god cannot choose to heal an individual if it lays within his sovereign will. The Christian should not demand or even expect healing but should seek God's will for their physical health and wellbeing entrusting their physical care as well as their spiritual care to the Lord.

1 Timothy Chapter 6: Instructions to Ministers

This is a major chapter in ones understanding of the role of the pastor in the local assembly; it provides an interesting picture of the attitude the pastor should have toward his own life and that of the congregation.

v.1 'Under the yoke'. This is a picture of an animal put to work in ploughing a field; it illustrates how the Christian is in a relationship with his master. Servant-hood is a key biblical principle and the church leader/pastor should lead the way in having a servant's heart. Each member of the body is called to a different aspect of the ministry, but all are simply servants ('deacons') to whom the Lord has entrusted a particular ministry (1 Cor. 12; Rom. 12:4–13). There is a beauty within the diversity of the people of God which should complement each member in order to see the Kingdom of God extended.

v.2 'teach and preach'. The whole content of this letter must be taught, as there are some very important truths contained within its pages. The able and trustworthy pastor must be able to preach the whole counsel of God (Acts 20:17–35 especially 20, 27 and 31–32). In ministry it is vitally important that the pastor dedicates time to Bible study and prayer for the purpose of building up the body of Christ (Eph. 4:12).

v.3 Paul again reveals his concern for the false teaching that was infiltrating the church; as a pastor, your attention must always be on the church in your care. A true shepherd cares for the flock by providing good food (biblical ministry) and by watching for the lion (the false teacher) who is set on disturbing the flock. The antidote for false doctrine is the truth which is found in Jesus Christ. The pastor/leader must be an individual who is fully aware of basic biblical doctrine in order to recognise the false teaching that will inevitably try and make its presence felt in the local congregation.

Note carefully the source of this false teaching—so called fellow Christians (Acts 20:29–30). It is important for the pastor/leader to be up to date with current trends in society; but not everything new is good and the pastor must be knowledgeable in matters of current affairs. Similarly, in a theological sense be sure that you do not accept all that is new as good—test everything against the word of God; but also be prepared to challenge tradition. Note the difference between Traditions which are biblical tenets which must not be changed and those traditions which are manmade and human imposed.

Be careful your academic studies do not replace your personal pursuit of growth in Christian grace.

v.6 Godliness or piety in religious observance or a good and holy life; is the vital element in the Christian life. The pastor must be content in life, not seeking fame and fortune but simply to please the God he serves.

v.7 Reminds the reader they can take nothing out of this world so why waste time and effort in accumulating the treasures of human desires but concentrate on the eternal nature of the divine being who will bring the ultimate fulfilment.

v.8 Food and clothing: the basic necessities in life should satisfy the pastor as he is engaged in higher activities than which the world offers (Acts 3:1–10; Phil.4:10–20).

The pastor should never:

i)   Be jealous of others.

ii)   Covet what others have.

v.10 The 'love of money' is a root of all evil, not money itself! A desire to gain from ones ministry or simply to be more than comfortable in life can cause much harm (v. 17). Here we are reminded of the intrinsic problem of trying to serve two masters (Matt. 6:24). In order to gain a correct perspective on material things the pastor/Christian should always look to the Lord as their example (Phil. 2:5–8).

v.11 The characteristics of the man of God—this is a vitally important subject for all potential pastors and leaders in the church.

1. *Righteousness. Justice and uprightness in all your dealings with men.*
2. *Godliness. A thorough conformity to the image of God and mind of Christ living a good and holy life.*
3. *Faith in Jesus, and in all that he has spoken; and fidelity to the talents thou hast received, and the office with which thou art intrusted.*

4. Love to *God and all mankind.*
5. *Perseverance. Patience in all trials and afflictions.*
6. *Gentleness. Bearing up with an even mind under all adversities and contradictions.*

Take time to examine the meanings of these words and understand how they can be related to your everyday experience as a Christian and then as a potential leader in the local church. Galatians 5:22–23 provides another helpful summary of these characteristics.

v.20 Here is a final personal plea from the author to Timothy; how good it is to have an experienced person guiding us through the pitfalls of pastoral ministry. Taking advice from older more experienced and godly people will help prevent problems arising in your own ministry.

I believe that the content of 1 Timothy is vital to all who are considering Christian ministry; it is also good at this point to stop and reflect upon your personal call to ministry; it is a serious issue, but one that is vital for the community in which you live.

Exercise: take some time to reflect upon your call to service whether that is full-time pastoral ministry or serving the local congregation in a 'lay' position. List below some of the issues and challenges you will face in your personal walk with God and as you lead the congregation in your care.

If you are currently in a pastoral role or considering this as a next step please give serious consideration to the call of God upon you; pastoral ministry is a serious business and should not be undertaken lightly. However if you are convinced of the call of God then be assured that he will equip and support throughout your pastoral ministry whatever the world, the flesh, or the devil may throw across your path.

2 Timothy: Paul's Last Words
Key Verse: 2 Tim. 1:13–14

- **Chapter 1**
  - Greetings 1:1–2
  - Timothy's faith 1:3–7
  - Called of God 1:8–12
  - Loyalty to faith 1:13–18
- **Chapter 2**
  - Strong in grace 2:1–13
  - God's workers 2:14–26
- **Chapter 3**
  - Perilous times 3:1–9
  - Man of God 3:10–15
  - Word of God 3:16–17
- **Chapter 4**
  - Preaching the word 4:1–5
  - Paul's valedictory 4:6–8
  - Personal remarks 4:9–22

Introduction

'Retain the standard of sound words which you heard from me, in the faith and love which are in Jesus Christ. Guard, through the Holy Spirit who dwells in us, the treasure which has been entrusted to you.' (2 Tim. 1:13–14).

- Paul wrote to Timothy again with more practical advice and a personal appeal before the apostle's death.

- Most probably written from a Roman prison, 65–68 CE; these are the last recorded words of the Apostle Paul.

- Timothy was in Ephesus and the letter was possibly taken to him by Tychicus (4:12).

- Although the letter is tinged with sadness one can also hear Paul's triumph in the Lord's victory. Paul knows there is no hope of his acquittal in his trial but his ultimate victory comes through the Lord. He is therefore writing as if he may never see his great friend Timothy again.

- Paul's main purposes for writing were to ensure that Timothy preserved the apostolic doctrine, and to encourage Timothy to personal diligence in the faith.

Main themes

1. *Encouragement.*

2. *Equipping against false teaching.*

3. *Need to set an example to all people.*

In chapter two, Paul tells Timothy that he must:

- endure hardness.

- toil with a soldier's loyalty.

- have the self-discipline of an athlete.

- work as hard as a farmer.

Faithfulness to the Lord is the key to success (4:7); this is essential in order to:

1. remain loyal to the gospel.

2. warn against perilous times.

3. train people to continue in the faith.

4.   proclaim the truth.

As a minister of the Gospel Timothy must:

a.   Conduct himself in a proper manner (2:22–25).

b.   Warn against false teachers (2:11–14, 3:1–9).

c.   Avoid foolishness (2:23)

d.   Correctly handle the word of truth (3:14–17, 4:2).

e.   Have confidence in God – who will overcome (4:1)!

As the apostle Paul came to the end of his life and ministry, we see that his greatest desire was to ensure the Gospel he had tirelessly proclaimed would continuing gathering people into the Kingdom of God, and that Timothy should be faithful to this task.

What is your greatest desire?

2 Timothy Chapter 1

v.1 Here is a personal greeting to a true friend and helper in the cause of the Gospel. This is the last recorded communication from the pen of the Apostle Paul; note here that Paul says he is an 'apostle' due to the 'will of God'. We cannot make ourselves anything, but our call comes from the Lord by grace.

What is an apostle? An apostle is 'someone sent with a commission/authority'.

v.3 Paul thanked God. Are we thankful servants? Are you happy to serve?

Constant prayers; do you pray regularly?

v.4 Here we see the emotion of a great man of God; as Jesus showed in John.11:35, there is nothing wrong with emotion!

v.5 Here we see the importance of a good biblical family upbringing. What kind of example do you give your family? 'Sincere' means genuine; the faith in Timothy's family was contagious, it was passed on from one generation to another. Passing on our faith to our children gives them a good foundation in life. Are you careful to maintain a good Christian standard among your family?

v.6 Although Timothy had a good background it is God's gift which is within the individual which allows for true involvement in ministry.

Timothy was to 'stir up' the gift of God—to keep in full flame the work that God had given him to do. The gift mentioned here is probably the gift of pastoral ministry (Eph. 4:11); this is a spiritual gift for the blessing of the congregation. Pastors are gifts to the church and as such have a responsibility to keep the ministry functioning (2 Tim. 4:5). Timothy was a pastor, but his ministry included other aspects of ministry such as evangelism, which is at the heart of the church.

v.7 Timothy lacked confidence, he was a timid man (1 Cor. 16:10; 1 Tim. 4:12). He was young, inexperienced, and timid, but it is ultimately God who gives us the power to carry out God's work. Never approach a problem by thinking of the size of the problem—instead think of the size of God!

v.8 At the time he wrote to Timothy, Paul was a prisoner, probably in Rome; we should be pleased to help all believers in difficult situations like this (Gal. 6:10; Philemon 1:7).

v.11 - Paul's self-description; preacher, apostle, teacher of the gospel:

- ➢ preaching – this was his public ministry.
- ➢ teaching – this was more private interaction.
- ➢ apostle – peripatetic; he travelled.

It is important to be sure of the role God has called you to and to stick at that task even when it becomes difficult (v. 16–18 Onesiphorus was a tireless worker who did not give up).

v.12 I am persuaded/I know. I was and I still am convinced that God is in control every day. Paul knew judgement would face every person his implicit trust in God was for the eternal care of his soul; that which had been entrusted to God at conversion. As Paul was facing the last weeks of his life he had an inner confidence in God's sovereign will to keep him through all the future trials on earth and bring him to his eternal reward.

v.13–14 These are essential instructions for the young pastor: sound words, faith and love. Deepening our knowledge of the word of God helps us to increase our faith and love will cause us to become more Christ-like. How we view the gospel will affect how we use it; Paul believed the gospel was a 'treasure' something of value that required careful handling.

Question: What is your view of the gospel? Do you perceive it as a special treasure that needs to be protected from false teaching and given to people as a precious gift?

v.16-18 There are always helpful people around who assist the preachers/missionaries in the practical issues; hospitality given to fellow disciples is an essential aspect of the activity of the Christian community. Onesiphorus was probably a resident of Ephesus a member of the church but someone who had travelled to Rome – possibly on business – and whilst there searched for Paul who was under arrest. He was not concerned with his own safety but simply in ensuring the well-being of the Apostle.

Timothy Chapter 2: A Good Soldier

v.1 'My son'; Timothy was not Paul's physical son, but he was his spiritual son.

Like Timothy so we too must 'be strong'—not in our strength but solely in the strength of God's grace. Our ability comes through Christ (Phil. 4:13).

v.2 Like Timothy we have a responsibility to carry on the work of teaching the message of the Bible.

'entrust' means to commit, like a deposit being placed in your account. We have to guard it this deposit (1:14). All pastors must be extremely careful with their Gospel. The message can easily become corrupted and become the words of man—a major reason why Paul wrote the Pastoral Epistles was to prevent this—avoid human philosophy and concentrate on God's word.

     i.   We need to learn in order to pass the baton on to others.

     ii.   We must be faithful in learning the truth.

     iii.   We must find other faithful people who can be trusted with the treasure of the gospel.

     iv.   We must be looking for leaders and prepared to mentor, guide, help, instruct and prepare them for the great responsibility of leadership.

Succession planning is essential in the local church; who will take on the work after you depart? A large amount of leadership issues would be avoided if there was more emphasis placed on succession planning and preparation of the next generation of leaders. True biblical leadership should be proactive and not reactive. The leaders should be looking to solve the problems before they arise; reactionary leadership tends to allow a fragmentary model that deals with issues when perhaps it is too late. Also if one tends to reactionary leadership the church does not understand the vision of the leader for the congregation. Such leadership portrays a lack of serious intent and positive strategic planning. Vision and planning go hand in hand if the leaders have a strong vision which is passed on to the church community then there will be less complaints, problems, issues and hence reactionary leadership decisions.

v.8 Here is the distinctive aspect of the gospel—the resurrection. If the resurrection is denied then there is no true power in the message that Christ is victorious over sin and death; yet amazingly from the very beginning of the gospel the resurrection was denied by some people (Matt. 28:11–15; cf. Rom. 1:1–4).

v.10 Despite all our troubles, our faith in Christ will be worth it in the end, as the goal or prize of our faith is salvation.

v.3–13 Paul had found contentment in his position in life; so must we despite:

> a.   Hardship v. 3; *suffer trouble during ones ministry.*
> b.   Labours v .6; *work hard and feel fatigued.*
> c.   Trouble v. 9; *experience hardship, suffer troubles.*
> d.   Bonds v. 9; *imprisonment.*

This is an aspect of the gospel that many do not want to hear, as it is not a popular message, however it is an inevitable part of the gospel experience especially for Christian leaders. In this section Paul refers to different people and their work experience and he draws the picture of the Christian minister.

v.3 soldiers; concentrate completely on the commands of their leaders; so too the minister should concentrate on serving the Lord and listening to the commands from the Master.

v.5 athletes; must train and follow the rules; there is no quick path to success; the minister must continue to walk the narrow path that leads to life as they endeavour to invite others and build up the congregation.

v.6 farmer; hard work epitomises the life of a good farmer; if they desire to produce a good crop and benefit from it they must be prepared to put in the hours of labour before the crops are planted; tend them as they grow and work at the harvest. For the Christian minister there are many stages to successful ministry. Firstly deep thoughtful study of the word of God. Secondly sowing the word of God in the community to i) build up the congregation and ii) to invite others to follow the gospel. Thirdly people need care if they are to grow spiritually and produce spiritual fruit; remember Eph. 4:12 the role of leaders is to equip the congregation to be more involved in service or ministry. Church is not to be a 'one man show' it is to be the true function of a body working in harmony to make progress.

v.10 provides the reason the minister should be willing to face all these difficulties; that others may know salvation and experience eternal glory.

Personal Conduct
This is an essential aspect for one's development as a minister of the gospel!

v.15 provides a summary:

> *Diligence in study – be earnest in your work, make haste.*
> *Approved – examined/tested to be correct.*
> *Workman – a labourer a doer James 1:22.*
> *Ashamed – having no cause for shame or embarrassment.*
> *Handling accurately – 'to cut straight' to divide rightly.*

One must pay careful attention to how one interprets the word; hence hermeneutics and homiletics (i.e. interpretation and explanation) are essential. True exegesis is essential in the delivery of the message of the scriptures. Beware of eisegesis, which is the kind of personal interpretation of the Bible that does not represent the true message of the passage being examined.

It is imperative that the student/pastor/preacher/teacher understands the context of the chapter/verse/word which is being studied. This relates not simply to the context within the specific book but also to the particular cultural setting and the historical aspect of the writer and the readers/hearers.

v.22 We must have the correct perspective on our lives; righteousness; faith; love; peace should be the goals of our personal conduct.

QUESTION: How can one increase these characteristics?

v.24 This verse concerns the conduct of servants: if one examines these characteristics it will become apparent that the emotional and psychological characteristics have to be kept under control. Perhaps here we are confronted with the fact that by nature ones humanity needs to be supressed by the Spirit in order to be selfless and gentle. Pastors must set the example to people in the community by means of non-reactionary attitudes; not searching for confrontation; but demonstrating patience and gentleness. Coupled with these qualities is the pastor's necessity to be able to teach. It is through solid biblical teaching that the pastor can instruct the church in the principles that are necessary for true Christian growth. True teaching also leads to salvation; this should be the ultimate goal of all the ministry which the local church is involved.

2 Timothy Chapter 3: Difficult Times Ahead

This chapter is essential reading for the 21st century as the issues dealt with are very prominent today; the last days!

v.1 The 'last days' (Greek: 'eschatos') began with the birth of Christ and will culminate with his return. Note what the characteristics of people living in the last days will be. Christians should be very aware of the popular worldview and general mind-set of the current generation in order to interact on a more relevant level with the world outside the church.

v.2–9 There will be huge social, political and religious problems in the last days.

Consider the current situation in your country and think about how these words relate to it today.

QUESTIONS

How do you approach your current cultural, political and social situations in respect to:

1) Understanding society as a whole?

2) As the arena into which you must take the gospel message?

There will be a great apostasy or falling away in the last days.

v.5 People will have a form of godliness; no power just simply exterior religious observance.

The Medicine for the Church in these Difficult Times

v.14 To 'continue' means to remain/abide/await. Where or in what must we abide? In the things of God 'that you have learned from me'; that is, the truth of the gospel; the Holy Scripture. One's foundation in life must be the scriptures, but it is also good to learn from people of greater experience.

Who do you look to in your spiritual life for help, encouragement, advice or mentoring? It is good practice to have an accountability partner; someone to whom you can talk about the problems, challenges, difficulties, and vision in your ministry.

Whilst you are in college this is easier, since you have a support network of lecturers and chaplains. However, when you enter ministry you might find that you are on your own. In that instance you will need to find a reliable and godly accountability partner to help you in the work.

Why?

v.16–17 – Because of the value of the scripture:

i. *inspired – a divine source 'God breathed'.*
ii. *profitable – helpful and advantageous.*
iii. *teaching – source of knowledge.*
iv. *reproof – means of conviction/convincing argument.*
v. *correction – when we/church goes astray.*
vi. *righteousness – that which makes us like God and approved/accepted by God.*

Why?

Because all must be equipped, so that the 'man of God' becomes:

v.17 i) adequate (perfect – complete in every part).

ii) equipped (with everything necessary for life and ministry).

God's inspired word must be properly applied in order to equip others in the work of ministry (Eph. 4:11–12).

2 Timothy Chapter 4: Keep Preaching!

What is the responsibility of the pastor? It must be to continue to preach and teach the truth of the Gospel in its fullest form (Acts 20:17–32).

v.1 Remember who it is that you serve—God. He is the one who will hold you to account and the one who will judge the outcome of one's ministry.

v.2 We must preach, for this is the divinely ordained manner of proclaiming the message of the gospel. Therefore it is essential that we develop good preaching methods, so that in our ministry we may:

> a. *reprove – put to shame by proving someone wrong.*
> b. *rebuke – admonish strongly – find the fault.*
> c. *exhort – call to for encouragement and comfort.*
> d. *show patience – long-suffering/endurance/forbearance.*
> e. *give instruction – doctrine/teaching.*

All these are necessary aspects of pastoral ministry—be sure to cover all of these aspects within your preaching and avoid being a one subject preacher. As Christians (and especially as ministers of the gospel) we are entrusted with the whole of the Word.

v.3–4 Some people leave true teaching and follow after people who make them feel good. Paul says that such people have 'Itching ears', for they love people who tell them what they want to hear, and not those who tell them what they need to hear. This can be a big temptation to preachers-we must be careful not to focus on making the people 'feel good' but focus on the truth. Remember the pastor/preacher/teacher is God's representative, and so we must give his word and not ours. Do not use the pulpit as an opportunity to simply share your views, but always as an opportunity to pass on the truth of the Gospel message.

> QUESTIONS
> 1. What issues do you face in respect of opposition to preaching the gospel from within the church?
> 2. How can these issues be dealt with?

Paul's Last Will and Testament

The Apostle's final words:

v.5 Still encouraging Timothy to keep working, Paul shows that evangelism is another essential aspect of pastoral ministry. Balance in ministry is essential, and the local pastor must have a heart for the community!

v.6–8 From these verses we understand that Paul had a definite hope in God's salvation; can we, like Paul, say that we have 'kept the faith'?

v.9–21 These verses contain personal matters and greetings.

Paul had influenced many people during his ministry.

Note v. 10 Demas was lost/left/backslidden. There is much debate about the spiritual condition of Demas; the general views are: i) He was not a true convert; I wonder if Paul would have allowed a non-Christian to accompany him on his missionary journeys? ii) He totally lost his faith; this would prove difficult to those who believe in 'once saved always saved'. iii) He couldn't handle the pressure of ministry and left to follow a less difficult lifestyle. I submit this is the most likely interpretation and proves that people should never enter in to Christian ministry unless they are convinced of the call of God upon their lives. Ministry cannot be carried out in one's own strength but only through the strength and knowledge of the Lord.

Note v.11 Luke was a companion of Paul. Mark, who had once left the work of God, had returned and was now profitable to Paul (Acts 15:36–41) don't give up on people there is always hope of restoration.

v.16–17 Paul had experienced the strength of God to face opposition against the faith. People will often let us down, but God is always faithful to his servants.

v.22 Paul ends his letter with a blessing!

2 Timothy is a personal letter tinged with sadness due to the imminent and impeding martyrdom of the Apostle Paul; however he did not concern himself with that. Instead, his driving ambition was to see the church established on a strong foundation for the next generation.

Titus: The Hope of the Gospel

Key verse: Titus 3:8

- **Chapter 1**
  - Greetings 1:1–4
  - Elders 1:5–9
  - Minister's responsibility 1:10–16
- **Chapter 2**
  - Sound teaching and conduct 2:1–10
  - Saving grace 2:11–15
- **Chapter 3**
  - Salvation and sanctification 3:1–8
  - Dissension and dispute 3:9–11
  - Greetings 3:12–15

Introduction

Looking for the blessed hope and the appearing of the glory of our great God and saviour Jesus Christ (Titus 2:13).

- Paul writes to Titus in order to guide this young man in the pastoral work he is engaged with on the island of Crete. Chronologically Titus should precede 2 Timothy however in the Biblical Canon Titus is set as the last of the three Pastoral Epistles.

- Titus' main purpose is to set the church in order and provide a solid foundation of leadership for future generations (1:5).

- Paul gives practical directions and encouragement to his young associate (1:4).

- It is generally accepted that the letter was written approx. 65 AD, possibly from Rome or somewhere in Macedonia.

Main themes

1. *Oppose false teachers.*
2. *Administer church affairs in a biblical fashion.*
3. *Beware of your personal conduct.*
4. *Hope of the return of Christ.*

Titus had 4 main reasons for being on the island of Crete:

1. *To appoint elders (1:5).*
2. *To expose false teachers, probably early Gnostics and Judaizers (1:10).*
3. *To edify/build up the church (2:1ff.).*
4. *To deal with false teachers in the church (3:9–11).*

Main theology:

a) *Election/salvation (1:1, 3; 2:10–11).*

b) *Redemption (2:14).*

c) *Ecclesiology (1:5, 7).*

d) *Eschatology (1:2; 2:13; 3:7).*

- The apostle Paul was nearing the end of his life and appears to have his mind focussed on eternal matters. The epistle to Titus shows us that every Christian should be looking to that day when Jesus will again reveal himself to the world! Although a short letter compared to 1 & 2 Timothy, it I full of helpful instruction and advice for a young pastor/church dealing with the pressing issues of the current situation.

Titus Chapter 1

v.1-2 Paul's introduction; a 'bond servant' is someone who has no rights of his own. This ministry has a fourfold aspect:

        a.   *Faith.*
        b.   *Knowledge.*
        c.   *Godliness.*
        d.   *Hope.*

The pastor/leader serves for the benefit of other people; it is important to remind ourselves often of the purpose or reason for one's ministry.

v.3 The message of the gospel has been 'entrusted' to those who preach, therefore it is essential that we guard it as a precious commodity and do not abuse one's responsibility.

v.4 'son' Titus was Paul's spiritual son, as was Timothy (1 Tim. 1:2; 2 Tim. 1:2). Paul had a great concern for the well-being of his spiritual son; God places a huge responsibility on those who look after others in the faith.

'Grace and peace'. These two attributes of God are things which the individual can benefit from; we can only receive these from the correct source—God.

v.5 Titus was to appoint elders in Crete, a small Mediterranean island. There is difficulty in placing Paul in Crete for the purpose of ministry. The only reference is found in Acts 27 as Paul was en-route to Rome as a prisoner; the vessel carrying him and other prisoners stopped in Crete. There is no record that Paul planted a church during this time however he may have left Titus there to commence the work. Another possibility is that Paul was released from his first Roman imprisonment when he travelled to Spain possibly returning to Jerusalem via Crete before his re-arrest and eventual execution. The Acts account holds many difficulties to the timing of the writing of the PE; however from this verse it is safe to assume that sometime during Paul's ministry he visited Crete and established a church or at least found a church that required organisation. In order to give the church on a solid foundation correct biblical leadership was essential. This is an important and difficult task for the pastor, as there is a need to ensure that the church is set on biblical foundations. That is why these epistles instruct sound doctrine and teaching—these are essential for healthy church growth. Often a pastor will be confronted with a disorganised and dysfunctional church, and how they set about reorganising and restructuring that church will affect the impact which the church makes in the community.

QUESTION: How would you start a restructure of a local church that was struggling with ministry, leadership, or outreach?

Church order was the responsibility of the pastor, whose role was to 'sort out the church'. In order to complete this task, the pastor had to be living in the correct spiritual relationship with God and setting a good example for the congregation. As the pastor grows spiritually, so the congregation will grow too, and the church will flourish. A point of interest here centres on the process used to select and install elders; here Paul instructs Titus to simply 'appoint' or ordain elders; there is no evidence of voting on new leaders. I submit it is the role of the pastor and elders to select suitable candidates for the roles as they have been entrusted with the spiritual leadership of the church. Sadly it is often the case that church members vote for personalities as opposed to truly understanding the spiritual nature of the roles. This can lead to the wrong people being in the wrong roles hence causing difficulties in the leadership of the local church.

v.6 For Titus' benefit, Paul lists the qualifications which those he appoints as elders must have these are the same as those in 1 Timothy. The elder must:

  i. *be faithful to his wife.*
  ii. *have an orderly family.*
  iii. *possess self-control.*
  iv. *not be someone who drinks alcohol, as this dulls the senses.*
  v. *be hospitable.*
  vi. *be able to teach.*
  vii. *not be greedy for money.*

These are serious issues and should be examined along with the similar lists in 1 Timothy 3:1-8. These requirements are necessary in order to maintain a strong and spiritual leadership within the local church. As you contemplate church leadership, how do you measure up to these standards? All of these attributes result from a close walk with the Lord. Leaders must set the example in spiritual life, commitment, diligence and desire. Any leader who does not set a suitable example should be removed from office.

v.10 Paul warns Titus against false teachers: a major theme of the Pastoral Epistles. There are those who are endeavouring to preach the gospel for their own gain and have selfish ambition as their motive.

'circumcision' – these were a group of Jews (Judaizers) who were endeavouring to impose their Jewish Old Testament laws on the new Christian communities; especially the rite of circumcision as being necessary for salvation. Syncretism is a major problem in the 21st century too, as people promote different gospels that contain all sorts of other religious rites, philosophies and humanistic thinking, along with a 'biblical' message. Often in the area of false teaching the differences are very subtle and well disguised. Paul then emphasises once again the necessity of solid biblical teaching in order to recognise false teaching and be able to combat its presence in the believing community.

QUESTION

Is syncretism an issue for you in your context?

If so, what are the main issues and how would you begin to deal with these issues in the church so that the true and pure gospel may be preached?

v.12 One of their own' is the Cretan poet Epimenides (c. 600 BCE); as seen here the Cretans were not the easiest people to pastor, lead and organise. Titus had a difficult task on his hands. Leadership is not easy! Often the leader is a lonely person because they endure criticism, questions, and doubts from others as well as inner doubts and fears. If you are contemplating becoming a leader then be sure that you realise it will be tough. In the Old Testament, Moses provides an excellent example of a leader who had difficult issues to challenge him; the majority of them were caused by his own people and sometimes by his own family (Ex. 14:10–12; 16:2; 17:2; 32).

In Exodus 18, Moses found it necessary to take good advice from his father-in-law, just as Titus needed good advice from Paul!

v.15 There is a requirement for the servant of the Lord to function in a pure and holy manner.

v.16 False teachers are often revealed by the way in which their actions and personal conduct are contrary to the biblical standards. Observing the behaviour of teachers and prospective leaders is essential; one should never rush to appoint a person to a role until they have proved their biblical basis and true Christian character. Often a person can be a different character outside of the church environment it is here that their qualities and faults can be more clearly observed. It is good practice to take to evaluate the message, means and motive of the person before accepting their teaching. One theme that Paul emphasises in the PE is that of care in selecting leaders and accepting teachers without giving them careful consideration.

Titus Chapter 2: Christian Duty

The author is endeavouring to mentor his young associate pastor and is keen to give him as much advice and help as is possible in this short letter. It is important that, as young leaders or prospective leaders, you seek out good advice from godly people who have experience of such work. Remember, you will never know everything and so it is imperative to carry on learning as you go through life.

A major theme of this epistle is that Titus must teach sound doctrine, especially in order to stand against false teachers.

QUESTIONS

What is sound doctrine?

Highlight the areas of Christian teaching you think are vital for the sound foundations necessary in the church.

v.2 These instructions for Christian living are relevant to all people for all time:

      a.   *Sensible living; dignified.*

      b.   *Holy living; no gossiping – tongue is a trouble maker!*

      c.   *loving living – love is the key to good Christian life and practice.*

      d.   *Set an example in your life style – however young you may feel!*

      e.   *Subjection in life – to those in authority but especially to Christ.*

v.12 The gospel instructs us to live:

      i)   A godly manner – doing what is right.

      ii)   And desire spiritual things and not carnal or earthly things.

      iii)   Seek righteousness or being acceptable before God; too often we are trying to please men when we should be concentrating more on pleasing God.

QUESTION: Why is personal conduct so important?

Titus supplies the answers:

v.5 So that the word of God is not dishonoured.

v.8 So that our opponents will have nothing bad to say against us.

v.10 It is a testimony to God's grace.

v.15 It is a means of building up and encouraging the church.

QUESTIONS

Do you realise that people are watching you?

Is your ministry relevant to all age groups?

Titus Chapter 3: Godly Living

v.1 'Remind them' leaders/elders and all Christians, just like those on Crete, all require to be constantly reminded of the necessity of godly living. We all need constant reminding of our Christian duty. *Is our purpose in life to be ready for every good work for the sake of the Kingdom of God?*

v.2 Be careful how you talk to people; never speak down to them but give everyone the consideration they deserve.

v.3 Why? Paul always gives his reasons behind his thinking. Good teachers, pastors/leaders must always explain themselves clearly and apply the point they are making. Application of the message is vital if the Christian community is going to grow. When we are speaking to others, especially the unsaved, remember that you too were once in the same situation and needed someone to help you understand the principles of the faith.

v.4 The 'kindness of God' is his benevolence, sweetness of disposition in spite of ingratitude.

'Brought' – this is a reference to our regeneration or salvation—we have been born again, made new in Christ; but regeneration is the door to holy Christian discipleship (Matt. 28:19 'go and make disciples').

QUESTIONS

What is the difference between seeking converts and making disciples?

What should a local pastor promote as necessary for true discipleship?

v.7 Another major theme of Titus is eschatology; and particularly the hope of the Second Coming. It is important to be aware of the 'signs' around us that relate to the end times. Was Paul feeling that his earthly existence was almost over and hence he had a greater appreciation of death and the prospect of eternity – often as young people there is little thought of eternity but it is an essential element of the New Testament gospel: preparing people for eternity. There are a few reasons for emphasising eschatology: i) Paul is looking forward to his eventual release to his eternal reward. ii) Paul is preparing Titus for the importance of this area of theology within the pastor's ministry. iii) There is a reminder to the Christian community of the urgency in evangelism. iv) A challenge to correct living in preparation for the church being taken up as the bride of Christ.

v.9–11 Avoid awkward men or false teachers. Again, it appears that Paul has the Judaizers in mind:

> a. *Genealogies were important to Jews.*
> b. *Law was essential to the Jews.*

v.12–15 Paul is sending help for Titus – in the work of the gospel you always need help from other willing people; do not make ministry an exclusive issue but be sure that you are aware of the body and its ability to compliment your ministry (1 Cor. 12).

It is important to know your weaknesses and be happy to accept outside help which will compliment your ministry and strengthen the church. Are you also willing to help rather than be the centre of attention?

v.15 Grace be with you, meaning, the favour of God be upon you.

The Pastoral Epistles are essential reading for all Christians but in particular for those in church leadership. These three personal letters are not a manual for church praxis; however they do give essential guidance to the pastor as how to approach some of the major issues they may face during their task of leading the people of God.

PROJECT: *Construct an outline for a discipleship course for use in the local church.*

Deal with:

# 1	What is discipleship?
# 2	Necessity of discipleship
# 3	Elements of true discipleship?
# 4	Write a brief outline of the major areas you would use to teach in a local church setting.

www.ingramcontent.com/pod-product-compliance
Lightning Source LLC
LaVergne TN
LVHW051710080426
835511LV00017B/2834

* 9 7 8 1 5 3 2 6 6 9 6 6 8 *